INSTAGRAM POETRY FOR EVERY DAY

Jessica Atkinson has been a social media manager
for arts organisations for the past decade. In her
role as Digital Content Manager at the Southbank
Centre's National Poetry Library in London,
she co-curated the world's first Instagram Poetry
exhibition in 2018.

Chris McCabe is the author of 12 books, and
many more collaborative and limited edition
publications. His work has been shortlisted for
the Ted Hughes Award and the Republic of
Consciousness Prize. He is the Head Librarian at
the Southbank Centre's National Poetry Library.

INSTAGRAM POETRY FOR EVERY DAY

Edited by Jessica Atkinson & Chris McCabe
National Poetry Library

Laurence King Publishing

SOUTHBANK
CENTRE

NATIONAL
POETRY LIBRARY

LAURENCE KING

Published by Laurence King Publishing Ltd
361–373 City Road
London EC1V 1LR
Tel: +44 (0)20 7841 6900
Email: enquiries@laurenceking.com
www.laurenceking.com

A catalogue record for this book is available from
the British Library.

ISBN: 978-1-78627-715-2

Commissioning editor: Jo Lightfoot
Design: Florian Michelet
Picture research: Ida Riveros

Printed in China

Laurence King Publishing is committed to
ethical and sustainable production. We are proud
participants in The Book Chain Project®
bookchainproject.com

CONTENTS

Introduction

Instagram Poetry for Every Day brings together work by poets who are using the platform to share poetry written in various, often contrasting styles and genres, many of whom have no similarities with each other than that they use Instagram as a way of sharing their work.

If there is one connecting factor between the poems presented in this book, it is visuality: most of the works here are meant to be engaged with as combined visual and textual entities. Instapoets repeatedly talk of Instagram as providing a gallery space in which they can curate their posts by, say, theme or colour, or even revel in randomness. There is one aspect, however, that connects them all: photography. Whatever the medium used to create the work – from paper to object – it is through photography that it will reach an audience. There is something radical in how the advancement of smartphones has allowed us all to become photographers. In the world of poetry this had led to the development of 'photopoetry', a genre that was invented by the Victorians and was first defined in 1935. Michael Nott writes in his book *Photopoetry* that 'the relationship between poem and photograph has always been one of disruption and serendipity, appropriation and exchange, evocation and metaphor.' Instagram poetry as visual form – melding text with image – revels in this disruption and serendipity.

Instagram, like the page, is not a fixed environment but an open space inviting experimentation and invention. Just as a poet might decide to appear at a live reading of their work, then allow the same work to appear in *Poetry Review*, Instagram provides another dimension, available for every poet and reader of poetry to engage with. It is a creative playing field for words to be reimagined in an instantly shareable medium. And just as poems have changed forms through the development of printed materials, from the standard two columns of medieval vellum to the wider possibilities of the trade edition, it is easily conceivable that Instagram and other digital technologies will begin to alter poetic form itself.

Poetry sales have doubled over the past decade with Rupi Kaur, the most famous Instapoet on the planet, leading the way. Published in 2014, Kaur's *Milk and Honey* had sold 1.4m copies by May 2017, which averaged slightly more than one copy per each of her followers. Since then, thousands of new poets have emerged on Instagram, garnering massive followings, which have led to publishing deals and lucrative sales. Many of those poets are in this book, showing that the digital and print worlds are very much in harmony: abundance in one area leads to abundance in another. This recent rise in Instagram poetry, or Instapoetry, has undeniably created an irritant in the breeches of poetry's gatekeepers.

But why all the fuss? Surely any platform that increases the visibility of and potential for engagement in poetry should be celebrated? Not so for Insta's critics. Various writers have attacked the lack of finesse in Instapoetry, the lack of engagement with tradition, its simplicity and focus on 'honesty'. Yet what this criticism confuses is the often 'simple' poetry that is presented on Instagram, with Instagram as a platform for poetry of all kinds. Instagram offers space for poetry written in every genre, including nature poetry, found poetry, conceptual poetry, love poetry, political poetry, lyric poetry, collage poetry, typewriter poetry, erasure (or 'blackout' poetry), sonnets and haiku. It has become a platform for poets who are also accomplished and celebrated in other areas of the artform, on the page for example, as well as the stage. Spoken word poets have found Instagram to be a powerful vehicle for expression, and a new generation of visual poets are fulfilling the hopes of the concrete poetry movement of the 1950s and '60s in creating a truly international community for their work.

The role of the National Poetry Library (NPL) is to celebrate poetry in all its forms; our collections exist as a national documentation of what we have come to know as poetry since 1912. In the spring of 2018 the NPL put out an international call for instapoems, offering the chance to be part of the world's first exhibition of Instagram poetry. The exhibition ran for nine weeks and received media attention from the *New York Times* and *Dazed and Confused* magazine.

As we dipped our toe into the sea of Instagram poetry, what became clear was that we were connecting with a huge community of active artists and prolific poets, some sharing multiple works every day. We had the chance to ask each of the poets featured in this book some questions about their work and their experiences on Instagram. While there were of course some points about the darker side of social media, there was continuity across a lot of the poets' answers as they explained how the Insta community had uplifted and validated their work. Many mentioned the instant feedback the platform offers to be of immense value, and although 'Likes' may seem at first a reductive measure of critique, sharing work and connecting with an online audience had allowed many of these poets to refine their output. Instagram has no borders, allowing many of these poets to grow an international following without ever having to board a plane. The platform has empowered creatives and democraticized the traditional processes, removing any need for the hierarchy of publishing houses or for gallery curators, and this is undeniably allowing new and important voices to emerge.

The NPL exhibition led to the creation of this anthology (incidentally, another world-first!). The very nature of Instagram poetry is variety, and that can be seen in the wide-ranging styles and forms within this book. The works are grouped by theme so although there may appear to be a patchwork effect at first, as you spend time with the poems you will uncover their common ground. This arrangement hopes to represent the sometimes frenetic, always diverse experience that Instagram poetry offers. Whether you're a devotee of scrolling, or discovering the genre afresh, this anthology provides insight into what makes a successful Instagram poem and explores what these works can tell us about life in the digital age.

I.

ASPIRATIONS

A huge part of the success and popularity of Instagram poetry is its ability to attract the scrolling reader. That instantaneous moment where the eyes cannot resist resting, reading and absorbing. This is the power of the form, not just on Instagram but across poetry, when a quiet reflection is distilled into words and makes sense of the world around us. Aphorisms have been described as 'small journeyings between poetry and prose' (Sharon Dolin), and Instagram is proving to be the vehicle for this new age of the aphorism to reach a wide audience.

@harmonivalentine.art

@harmonivalentine.art When it comes to how I blackout the poem, I'm inspired by organic and repeating patterns. I like seeing the design 'grow' onto the page. After I've found the words to the poem, I enjoy getting lost in the repetitive designs as a way to meditate and relax.

A naive peace

in the belief that one day

it'll all make sense.

I think we tuck ourselves

into beds made of this,

these soft sheets of some

far off time

where everything we ached for

is wrapped up sweet and tight

in the color of understanding.

What's this for if not this?

There must come a passing

to the storm.

—Tyler Knott Gregson—

@tylerknott

@tylerknott Writing for me is a pressure release, and so the quicker I can get the thoughts out, the better I feel. I do notice that when I shift away from the keyboard to typing on the typewriter, it slows me down, bringing me back to the tangible, and I appreciate it.

Wild Embers

We are the descendants
of the wild women you forgot
We are the stories you thought
would never be taught.

They should have checked the ashes
of the women they burned alive.
Because it takes a single wild ember
to bring a whole wildfire to life.

―――――

Nikita Gill

Wild Embers • **@nikita_gill**

@nikita_gill My mother read me mythology and folklore as a child before she read me fiction or children's books. This sparked my interest in the gods and goddesses and other archetypes. I frequently imagine those archetypes in the modern day.

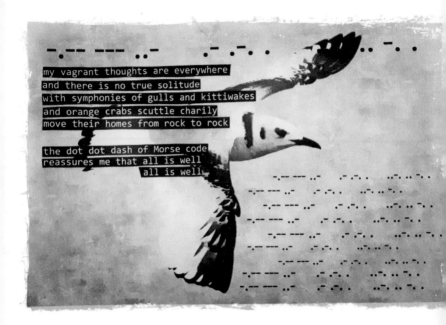

my vagrant thoughts are everywhere
and there is no true solitude
with symphonies of gulls and kittiwakes
and orange crabs scuttle charily
move their homes from rock to rock

the dot dot dash of Morse code
reassures me that all is well
all is well

@ravingpoet64

@ravingpoet64 Usually what I'm reading feeds into my work – Greek myths, nature writing, politics, etc. 'Atlas of Cursed Places' and Ann Carson's poems have been big influences this year.

@robertmontgomeryghost

@robertmontgomeryghost I think it's poetry's job to try to uncover the beautiful in the everyday; to find hidden magic in the mundane, and to help make us feel as alive as possible.

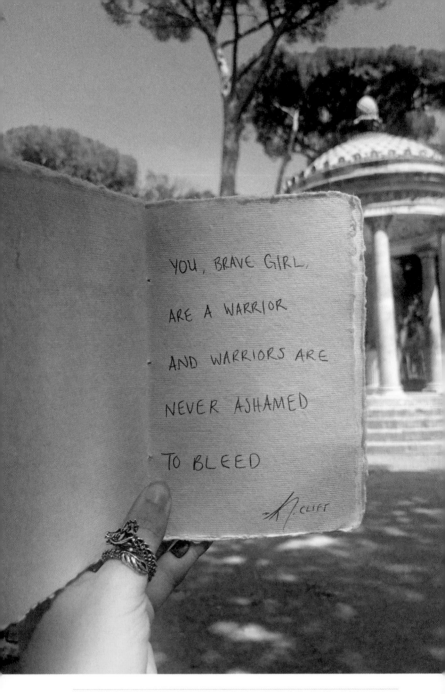

@anon_sense

6. Tempest Intentions

Tis better to have
felt immortal and a fool
than to never have

@hmsgordon

@hmsgordon I write and perform all kinds of poetry. Haiku is the first traditional form I got into. One of the key features of a haiku is that it should not rhyme; that step away from rhyming has helped my writing to develop.

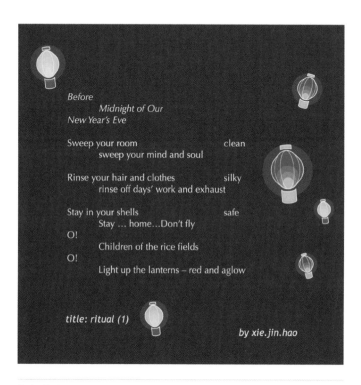

Before
          Midnight of Our
New Year's Eve

Sweep your room   clean
          sweep your mind and soul

Rinse your hair and clothes   silky
          rinse off days' work and exhaust

Stay in your shells   safe
          Stay … home…Don't fly
O!
          Children of the rice fields
O!
          Light up the lanterns – red and aglow

title: ritual (1)

                                   by xie.jin.hao

@xie.jin.hao

@xie.jin.hao I don't think Instagram influences my poems as such. I think of Instagram as a vessel or a carrier for my poems to be read by others and to connect with them in a timely manner.

II.
CREATIVITY

It's what the platform was built for: there is no denying the outpouring of creativity across all art forms that Instagram has enabled over the past decade. You can find so many genres of poetry brought to life on Instagram – visual poetry, blackout poetry, poems that manipulate space and form. It's a place to be playful and experiment, with limitless possibilities (as long as you can photograph whatever you've created!), and the democracy of social media allows entry to those who might not have previously thought of themselves as artistic, to become such.

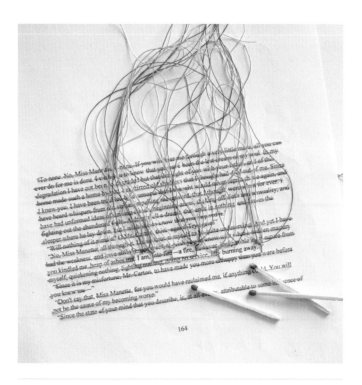

@foolishfancy

@foolishfancy I've found that the poetry and the words are only half the story, and Instagram allows me to tell the rest of it in photo form. The right props, lighting or shadow captured in a photograph complete the story.

i write myself into
forgotten places.
the corners
of empty apartments.
the last sip of wine
left in the sun.
the remnants.
i write until i
am a forgotten place.
i write until i
am forgotten.

i write until
i am.
i write until.
i write.

i am.
am i

@alison.malee

 @alison.malee I read to understand. Novels, poetry. The world is grand and vast, and I think the more we try to understand it through our art, the more we understand ourselves.

@lucialitman

@lucialitman Sometimes I'm just not inspired, and I remind myself that that's okay. Creativity for me isn't an endless stream, I have to make sure I'm getting enough rest and time to recharge my creative juices away from my phone and away from others (I'm an introvert).

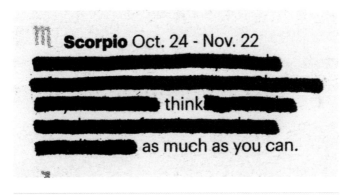

Scorpio Oct. 24 - Nov. 22

██████████████████████████

████████████████████████████████

█████████████ think█████████████

██████████████████████

█████████████ as much as you can.

@hiddenhoroscopes

@hiddenhoroscopes I wouldn't say that my horoscopes are attempting to predict anything, rather just offering a simple word of advice. It's fun and challenging to pull a few words out of some sentences and form them into little messages. I don't think I could predict more than a few seconds into the future.

she went looking for
a lighthouse
and found herself
instead;
now, she can light
the way for others.
- the poetry bandit

@the_poetrybandit

@the_poetrybandit I became the Poetry Bandit as I figured, since I was trying to write to distract myself from drinking all the time, I was really stealing my love of language and poetry from my addiction, which had in turn stolen it from me.

poetry

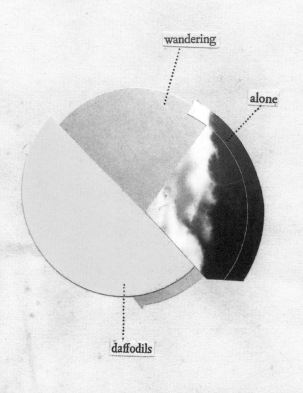

wandering

alone

daffodils

heart rate mimics a

Gramophone

Illustrate a section of breath

a cross stitched from lungs.

each a small prayer,

an act of transformation

THE FLIP OF A COIN

the rhythm of a well

traces along the ribs

I open and sound is me

every pore an amplifier

the blessing of a note   an act of breathing

@zahrah_s

@zahrah_s Poetry does help me reflect – explore a moment that I have lived. It helps me understand myself. It allows me to record and remix the feelings I have. You can capture the fleeting, you can capture the journey.

My   house
falls
like   the   House   of   Usher—
   desires split   like   hair   end,
the   chasm   runs   like   a   creek   .

A   choir   not   a   choir   cannot   acquire
the   future   that   it   needs
to   stop   the   kneading   of   briar—
a land slowly retires   in the loving arms of
campfires   that   are   not   campfires,
but   soul   songs   of   self-indulgent   liars.

We   hide
the   glass under the table along with
the   fables   we   suffocate.
We   sweep   our   lips   under   the   rug,   like
the   liliums   we   left   for   Abel.

@aft3rthought

@aft3rthought I enjoy working in between and across genres.
I bring elements of visual art into the literary through experimen-
tations with form, so that words and letters become performative
in the space of the page.

@postpoetical

@postpoetical I have always been interested in how poetry and visual art can combine, and Instagram brings those relationships into sharper focus for me. Now I find myself composing visually and verbally simultaneously; the poems and the images are together from the outset of composition.

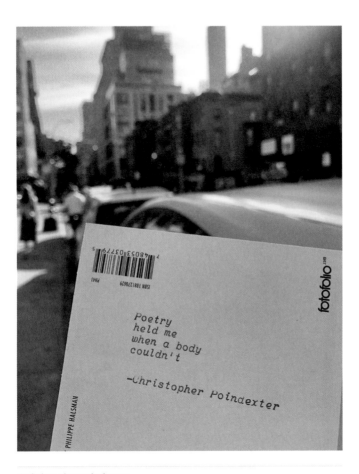

@christopherpoindexter

 @christopherpoindexter A lot of the same lines of mine get used for tattoos, most of them are rooted in the same thing – love. Love for self. Love for others. Love for the earth.

III.

IDENTITY

'I celebrate myself, and sing myself,
And what I assume you shall assume,
For every atom belonging to me as good
    belongs to you.'
- Walt Whitman, 'Song of Myself' (1855)

Poetry and the self have tended to go hand in hand for generations. While selfhood may be an age-old topic, the artistic conversation about identity has never been more vibrant, and the internet has played a huge part in that. It's important to recognize the visibility and representation that platforms like Instagram allow us. For some, the notion of identity has been taken for granted, while others have been denied that expression of self throughout history. In many parts of the world, social media has become the great leveller, bringing about a transferral of power to a new generation of storytellers and poets.

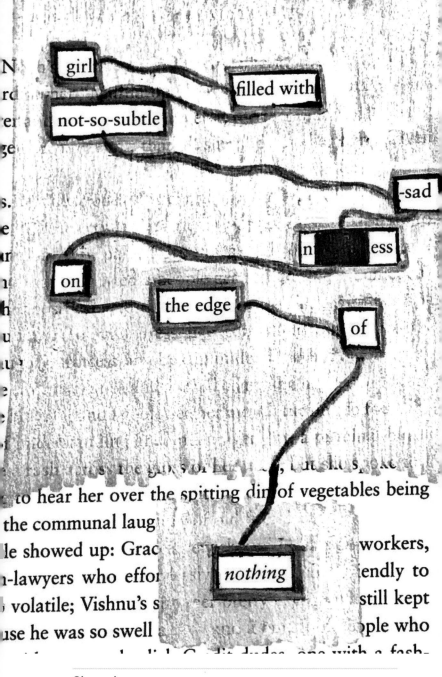

girl filled with not-so-subtle -sad n ess on the edge of nothing

to hear her over the spitting din of vegetables being
the communal laug
le showed up: Grac   workers,
-lawyers who effor   endly to
volatile; Vishnu's s   still kept
use he was so swell   ple who

| it is okay
to still be
putting
yourself
together |

ben maxfield

@bnmxfld

@bnmxfld I'm not sure I know what inspires me until it inspires me. There are times that I can go days, weeks even, without anything tickling the pieces of my soul. Then all at once, something reaches out to me.

@preschooldr0pout

@preschooldr0pout Sometimes it can be cathartic for me to find humour as I process mundane or even upsetting situations, and I think others can relate to that as well. Unexpected humour or lighthearted fun can serve as a nice break from everyday life and the world around us.

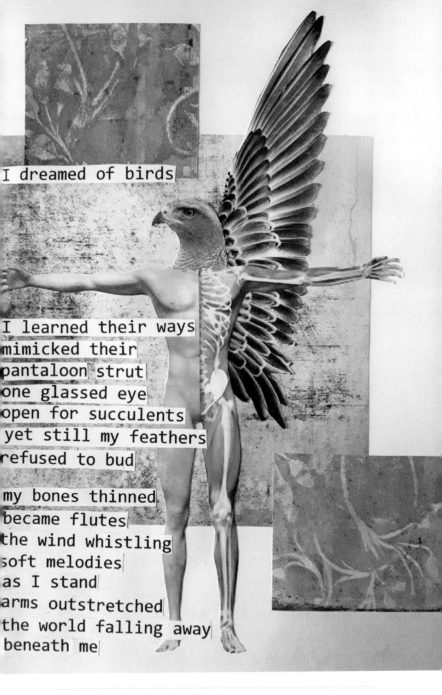

I dreamed of birds

I learned their ways
mimicked their
pantaloon strut
one glassed eye
open for succulents
yet still my feathers
refused to bud

my bones thinned
became flutes
the wind whistling
soft melodies
as I stand
arms outstretched
the world falling away
beneath me

@ravingpoet64

39

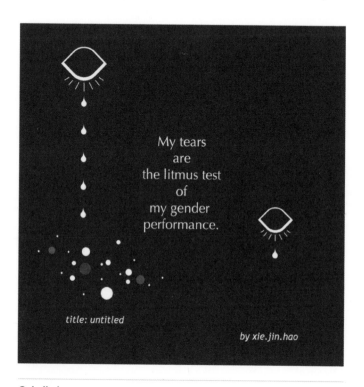

title: untitled

by xie.jin.hao

@xie.jin.hao

@xie.jin.hao Instagram allows me to express my poetics without any limitations. It allows me to experiment with forms and different topics without worrying if that poem would make it to publication. I use Instagram to record my poetic journey.

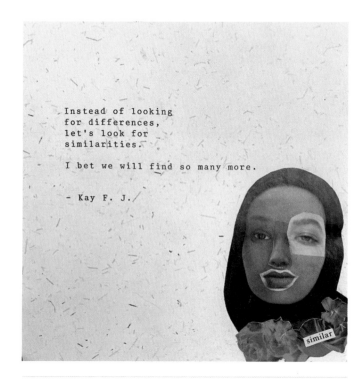

Instead of looking
for differences,
let's look for
similarities.

I bet we will find so many more.

- Kay F. J.

@kayf.j

@kayf.j Instagram allows you as an artist to evolve and to look back on that evolution through your feed. Having a free platform to share my thoughts has been such a blessing, and has allowed me to reach people all over the world. It's incredible!

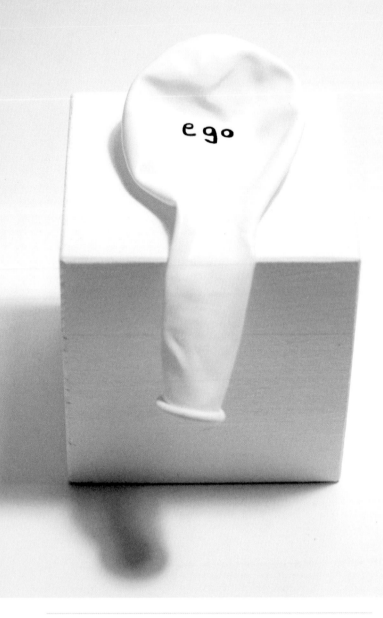

ego (2012) • **@anatolknotek**

@_paradoxandmetaphors_

@_paradoxandmetaphors_ Literary expression is a double-edged sword that impacts both the writer and the reader. All my inspiration is driven by the fact that words can add life to the seemingly irrelevant and there's always a new way to say the same thing.

Anatomy of a Sunday

Awake at 5:19am,
taste every drink of the previous night on my breath,
run tongue over furred teeth
and stare sticky-lashed at my phone screen;
Google image search Justin Trudeau,
half-heartedly masturbate.
Am very aware of the cobwebs on the ceiling fan
and the Amazon burning
and my dry lips.
Relish the snap and crunch of the ibuprofen blister pack;
swallow, swallow.

Drive to parents' house,
my mother hovers as I eat lunch:
tandoori chicken, chapatti, raita;
she tells me everything that is wrong with her life
and I swallow, swallow.
My father does not come in from the garden
and then asks me why I am leaving so soon,
two hours later.

3pm,
relief at being alone again;
sit at local bar and sip Aperol spritz,
watch the condensation drip down the side of my glass
and pool on the wooden benchtop,
watch the beautiful boy playing guitar on the stage,
plucking the strings as though they are stars –
singing as though he holds a galaxy in his mouth.
Am very aware of how I can take up so much space,
yet feel so small;
how every drop of me
fills the gaps in between every moment in time;
and I am struggling to breathe but I
swallow, swallow.

@the.part.time.poet

THE BOX SAID **"MALE"**, **"FEMALE"** OR **"OTHER"**.
"OTHER", AS IN TOO EXPANSIVE FOR THIS BOX.
TOO MUCH FOR THIS BOX TO CONTAIN.
TOO MANY WORDS, OCEANS, WEIGHTS OF PAST BODIES TO FIT.
HOW IS IT POSSIBLE FOR ME TO WRITE DOWN ALL THE WAYS IN WHICH
THIS WORLD HAS SCARRED ME,
ALL THE WAYS IN WHICH THESE BOXES HAVE BRUISED SKELETONS BEFORE MINE,
ALL THE WAYS THIS BOX HAS MURDERED BRILLIANCE IN THE NAME OF ORDER.

SO I LEAVE THE BOX BLANK.
CROSS LINES THROUGH IT.
PROTEST ON THE PAGE.
YET SOMETIMES, I FEEL THIS FITS US BETTER.
THE **GENDER AS A PROTEST**,
OUR **GENDER AS CROSSED LINES**,
MY GENDER IS SO OFTEN JUST AS BLANK, AS IT IS FULL.

@travisalabanza

@travisalabanza I try and focus on making the work that feels right …. I do think what we are seeing is a push from artists to make their own platforms, not wait for the door to open, rather to create our own doors.

IV.

HUMOUR

According to some, poets might be the last group of artists to make you laugh, but then look again at the track record of comedic genius in the poetic form: Lewis Carroll, Stevie Smith, John Agard ... the list goes on. Instagram has emerged as a platform for comedic poetry, which contains the added potential for visual elements to appear alongside the words. Whether it's a cartoon or well-timed photograph, Instagram poetry can provide a much-needed smile on even the most difficult of days.

Robert Frost's Netflix Choice

An action thriller
with Liam Neeson
or a post-apocalyptic
world forsaken?

Decides upon *The Road* not *Taken*.

@brian_bilston

 @brian_bilston Although I've always found Twitter to be more of a home for humour than Instagram, there is much humour and joy to be found on there; it's a great environment for cartoonists, comedians and, indeed, writers of supposedly comic verse.

10. The Future

Dating post-thirty:
like shopping in TK Maxx
A lot of effort

@hmsgordon

@hmsgordon Instagram gives me a way of instantly publishing my work. It was the chance of it being exhibited as part of the National Poetry Library's Instagram poetry exhibition that led me to post my haiku. I thought of it more as a submission, and collaborated with a friend, artist Michael Cox, to give my work a visualization beyond the words.

@postpoetical

@postpoetical I made a very deliberate decision to start posting work on Instagram to see if there was room for poetry that was a bit different, more oblique and experimental than most of what I was hearing about.

sand museum (2019)   •   **@davidbellingham_**

@davidbellingham_ The challenge of any prescribed format is to discover ways to make the most of its limitations. Not all works suit the Instagram format: longer form or more detailed pieces are not appropriate to the space. Instagram posts are ideal for regular updates of work in progress.

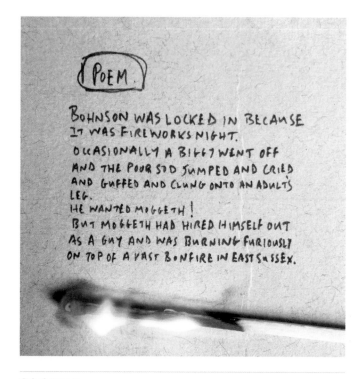

POEM.

BOHNSON WAS LOCKED IN BECAUSE
IT WAS FIREWORKS NIGHT.
OCCASIONALLY A BILLY WENT OFF
AND THE POOR SOD JUMPED AND CRIED
AND GUFFED AND CLUNG ONTO AN ADULT'S
LEG.
HE WANTED MOGGETH!
BUT MOGGETH HAD HIRED HIMSELF OUT
AS A GUY AND WAS BURNING FURIOUSLY
ON TOP OF A VAST BONFIRE IN EAST SUSSEX.

@timkeypoet

@timkeypoet There's no real story behind these two, I just imagined this Bohnson fella and got into a groove writing for him. Just this white-haired imbecile, waddling about, clueless like we all are. Then I thought he should have a friend (who I called Moggeth) who was cleverer than Bohnson but with no soul and the ability to change shape and pour himself into bottles.

@timkeypoet

@timkeypoet Once the basics were in place, they were fun to write for. I never discussed them on stage; they felt better left on Instagram, where I could keep an eye on them.

Vampire

ɞ

ɞ

blood

@lukebuserart

@lukebuserart Instagram is a really great way to get the word out about what I'm working on and to promote exhibitions. It's also good for getting feedback on projects.

I CAN'T EVEN BE MYSELF

BY MYSELF.

@aprilhillwriting

@aprilhillwriting I am inspired by this little feeling that becomes a voice inside my head. It tells me what to write and how to write it down. I just fill the words in and put them together on a piece of paper.

V.

LOVE

Since poets first began putting ink to paper, there have been poems about love. From Sappho to Chaucer, Emily Dickinson to Rabindranath Tagore, poets have risen to the challenge of trying to make sense of this most confusing, elating, tiring and bewildering of human emotions. Instagram poetry offers a very different approach to the traditional handwritten poem left privately for the beloved to read. These declarations of love are liked (red heart) by a mass audience almost as soon as they're written.

tell me
you love me
even if
you have to
cross your fingers
behind your back
while you
do it.

—amanda lovelace

@ladybookmad

@ladybookmad In any given day, I might be inspired by a book, a commercial, a Tarot card, a conversation, a single word. Everything has the potential to be turned into a poem, but only if you're paying attention!

four roses for you (2016) • **@anatolknotek**

I fell off my pink cloud with a thud

that cushion of champagne and diamonds
the yacht, a jet, furs purring in the close
and love, wayward and mercurial

Let me tell you
   - love was no soft landing

My love whose arms are the waterfall
necks of midsummer roses and
raincloud towers,
whose arms are the foreign
dictionaries of lovers
who own nothing but ideas of new
civilizations we still never reach.

@gretabellamacina

@gretabellamacina I think poetry is an eternal language.
It speaks from the grave up into the sky and down to our souls.
It has the power to speak to you even if you don't know you need it.

@mabebuart

 @mabebuart upright proud in
red patent high heel pumps
I go out into
that blue night
that preserves
my love

AND WE SHALL STEAL AWAY IN THE BLUE DAWN BY THE NOON SUN WE'LL BE FUCKING GONE

In last night's dream,
you drove me along on
cerulean blue of the Pacific
on a marigold Vespa;
the wind furled under our
salt & pepper hair
and
we were still in love.

paradox & metaphors

@_paradoxandmetaphors_

@_paradoxandmetaphors_ I love making both handmade and digital poems. I enjoy experimenting with both formats to add a sense of freshness to the account and also because the audience always likes something new.

I STOPPED
MISSING
OUR BLISS,
ONCE I REALIZED
IT WAS SCRIPTED

M A R Y A   L A Y T H

@marya.layth

@marya.layth It is impossible to pinpoint any one thing that inspires me. I do know that I write for my own well-being. To unburden me of myself. The magic of metaphor and the boundlessness of language happen to be powerful tools towards that end.

You're the tuck in, the promise
that the doors and windows
are locked up tight,
home like a safe house,
secure from the monsters
there must be out there

beyond it all.

You're the light switch flick,
you're the footsteps in the night

climbing up then down

wearing grooves in the staircase,
you're the white lie that brings comfort,
even though they know you're lying.

You're the ocean of patience and I'm still
a boat built too small to sail it,

bobbing in the swell, hands on rails
but trying my very best.

Teach me what you know of these currents,
show me the way to stay afloat.

-Tyler Knott Gregson-

66

@egysorosok

@egysorosok The real challenge for me is that Instagram is full of these fake happy-perfect lives. Most of us are in an invisible competition with others ... so I've decided that I would like to do something real on a platform which is mostly not real at all. I like the fact that I have to be short and punchy.

VI.

MENTAL
HEALTH

Poetry has often been seen as offering a form of catharsis, a kind of purging of emotions that can help make sense of an experience. True as this might be, the confidence of poets to openly publicize their most intimate thoughts and inner turmoils has provided some of the most powerful literature ever created. From Gerard Manley Hopkins to Sylvia Plath, poets have found words for their darkest moments, inviting readers into their private space. In this tradition, many Instagram poets don't shy away from presenting their personal life for public scrutiny, and in the context of social media, they do this very, very publicly.

@depressingfridgepoems

 @depressingfridgepoems What's wonderful about Instagram is that I can have a ridiculous idea and within minutes get it out to thousands of people across the world.

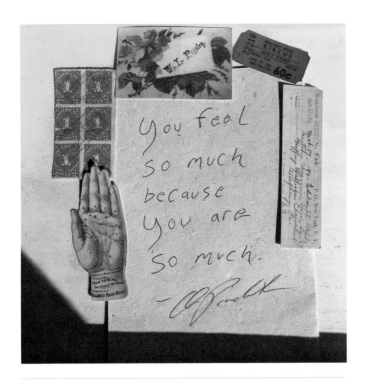

@christopherpoindexter

@christopherpoindexter Social media, like anything else, is both a blessing and a curse. I think if artists have the vision to use it as a tool to illuminate their most honest work, it can truly be an incredible thing.

| some of my
demons look
just like you |

ben maxfield

@bnmxfld

@bnmxfld My colour schemes are personal; when I'm writing about a particular person, and their favourite color might be blue, or green, I'll use a shred of paper or a fragment of glass that's the same colour. A piece of them, visually.

depression cherry.
like the sugar stained
cocktails
we sip.
satin sheets
dipped in
watercolour paints.
depression cherry.
the hue of
saints & surrender.
depression cherry
was red
before we remembererd.

ivy

@ivyatmidnight

@ivyatmidnight Sitting in the present and piecing a poem together is my favourite part of the day. It gives me the space to process any thoughts I've been burying and then I'm able to share those with an incredibly supportive community, often finding that others are experiencing similar feelings.

@preschooldr0pout

@preschooldr0pout When I make my collages it's first and foremost a meditative process. For me, collage poetry is a means of tapping into unconscious thoughts and feelings, and acts as a tool to express myself in ways I wouldn't otherwise be able to.

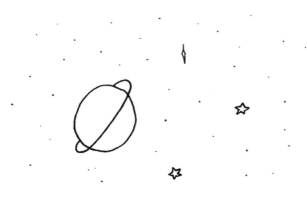

IF YOU NEED ME

I AM HERE,

IF YOU NEED SPACE

I AM GONE.

@aprilhillwriting

 @aprilhillwriting I see myself as a realist. I live in a black and white world that has a lot of rules. I try and find the good in everything but I also find myself feeling bad a lot of the time.

cages

are
still cages

even
when they're

designed
to

look
just like

castles.

—amanda lovelace

@ladybookmad

@ladybookmad I went from writing a very personal narrative to writing a political, community-driven book, and I'm not sure the latter would have existed if we hadn't been able to come together in our experiences because of platforms like Instagram.

@susieinmn

@susieinmn Instagram is an open stage on which I can perform and show up without any constraints other than those I put upon myself. It reaches my followers and hopefully inspires them in some way.

I'm s/or/ry t/h/at y/o/u did
not b/el/ie/ve me.
i'/m s/or/ry t/h/at this body
did not f/i/t vi/ct/im well.
i'm so/r/ry that t/h/is body
does n/o/t fit.

@travisalabanza

@travisalabanza Instagram was the only access point I had to create an audience. I didn't go to university, or art school, or grow up around artists. The art world DIDN'T wanna let me in, but on the internet I could create my own audience.

HE WHISPERED INTO YOUR EAR
"YOU MAKE ME FEEL LIKE I CAN BE MORE THAN A MAN"
YOU CARVED INTO HIS BACK
"WE ALL CAN, IT IS JUST ABOUT BREATHING"

HE CONTINUED TO CRY INTO YOUR BREAST TEMPLATE,
"WHEN WE KISS IT FEELS LIKE GENDER DISAPPEARS"
YOU SUNG BACK
**"DON'T THESE BODY PARTS LOOK SO MUCH BETTER
WITHOUT US?"**

HE GOT UP AND PUT BACK ON HIS ARMOUR AND STRAIGHTENED UP.
AND YOU REMEMBERED HANDS LIKE YOURS HAVE BEEN DOING
THIS WORK FOR YEARS.
SOMETIMES IT IS NOT LOVE THAT THEY CRAVE FROM YOUR TOUCH,
RATHER A THERAPY SESSION IN WHICH NO INVOICE IS EVER SENT.

@travisalabanza

@travisalabanza Often people discredit Instagram as a lower form of showing work – but to me that is because people discredit things that are accessible. Instagram has meant that my work can be seen across the world, with people of all ages, and be shared in a way that doesn't happen via physical space.

VII.
NATURE

'Who has seen the wind?
Neither you nor I:
But when the trees bow down their heads,
The wind is passing by.'
- Christina Rossetti, 'Who Has Seen the Wind?' (1872)

Many Instagram poets have made woodlands, forests and coastlines the most visible landscapes for their poems. Indeed, some often merge two forms that have historically been used to capture the natural landscape: poetry itself, and photography. In these posts we are presented with words and images from around the globe, and they bring us closer to places we might never experience directly.

how brittle,
this tender thing
we call creation.

alison malee

@alison.malee

@alison.malee Almost all of my creativity takes its shape as some form of writing. Once a poem is written, I usually pull a line or two and decide what sort of materials would be the most authentic and effective for that piece.

@bees__buzz

 @bees__buzz I'm inspired by everything! The world outside my window, being a mother, eating a good meal, hearing a new piece of music that makes me feel alive, or hearing a familiar piece of music that reminds me of a simpler time in life.

a clearing of sense in a forest of nonsense (2019)　•　**@davidbellingham_**

@davidbellingham_ My approach to the Instagram format has been to treat it as a refreshment of the simple printed picture postcard. On a postcard, image and text are placed on either side of a piece of printed card, while the basic Instagram post offers this duality of single image and short text.

four giraffes in a field

@lukebuserart

@lukebuserart I've never been good with computers and I've always preferred making non-digital art, so the typewriter has never seemed restrictive to me. There are many ways to manipulate the typewriter and the paper to achieve the pieces I make!

snow that blinds you
burns your scalp and eyelids
snow that makes halos

snow marked by wolves
snow that looks blue
in first light

snow used for exquisite
erotic rituals
drifts with the imprint
of crazy lovers

snow that never
reaches the ground

the idea of snow

@harmonivalentine.art

@harmonivalentine.art I began doing blackout poems during an emotional time in my life. I was inspired by how I could find the words to express myself on the page, even when it felt difficult to express how I was feeling. I'm inspired by words and poems that are strikingly emotional, strong, fierce and succinct.

THE OVERGROWN
GARDEN INSIDE
YOUR HEAD
DOES NOT DIE
JUST
BECAUSE
YOU
CLOSE
YOUR
EYES...

MARYA LAYTH

@marya.layth

@marya.layth I am acutely aware that the face ages and changes with time. The way we look is too unstable to be attached to. It is why I want to identify with and be seen for my art more than anything else.

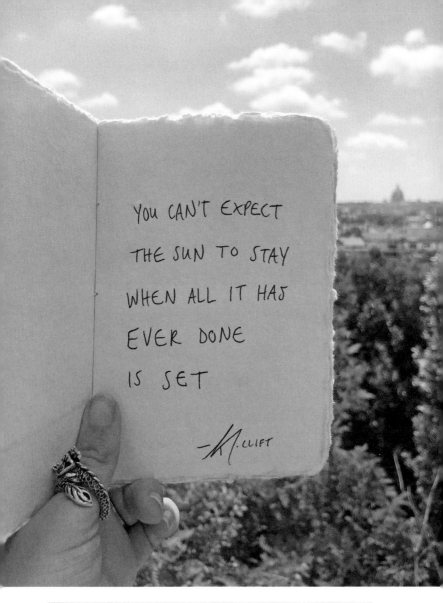

YOU CAN'T EXPECT
THE SUN TO STAY
WHEN ALL IT HAS
EVER DONE
IS SET

—K. CLIFT

@r.cliftpoetry

@r.cliftpoetry There is a community of poets that I am lucky to be a part of, and we have worked together to make our corner of social media a safe place for writers and readers to be vulnerable with their words. I've built a loving, loyal following on Instagram. They give my heart a place to be heard, and for that I will always be grateful.

@anon_sense

 @ anon_sense There's an entire community of writers and artists supporting and uplifting each other. No one cares what you look like, where you live, your economic status, etc. Everyone is equal in their art form.

The Catching

We hold our hands
out of car windows,
receiving rain
with curled fingers
and telling ourselves
that the release
is in the catching.

A skeleton leaf
jitterbugs
across two lanes of traffic.

I swerve to avoid it,
and the freedom is in the moment
I visualise the three-car pile-up
that never happens.

We listen to the rain
from bed,
drink our tea
and reassure each other
that we are better off dry.

@the.part.time.poet

@the.part.time.poet Sometimes I think a poem may be too personal or specific for others to relate to, yet often those can end up being incredibly popular. I have also learned that there is magic in the ordinary; that events and interactions that might otherwise be considered mundane can be a portal to something deeper.

VIII.
SOCIETY

From its beginnings, each age has had its politically engaged poets. From the early Greeks through to Shakespeare, poets have thrived on revealing and (sometimes) vaguely concealing what they think about the powers that be. While specific political events are often quickly forgotten, we still return to the work of poets who remind us that 'Revolution is not a one-time event' (Audre Lorde). Instagram is alive with probing, questioning minds that use the digital platform to speak truth to power. From the climate emergency to capitalism, you'll find poems that confirm or challenge your world view.

human right$ (2012) • **@anatolknotek**

@anatolknotek I think that concrete poetry nowadays cannot have the same impact as when it was invented. But every form of art changes over time, and I see my work as a child or grandchild of these works.

look how language cleaves us in half

看语言把大家切开来

when you are not willing to learn about others

当你不愿去了解其他

title: no.11

by xie.jin.hao

@xie.jin.hao

@xie.jin.hao Mostly I am interested in stretching out the canvas of language as a tool or conveyor that dictates our experience of the world: how it can bridge us, but also divide us as a human collective.

THE GROUND IS STREWN WITH DEBRIS

THE AIR IS THICK WITH HUBRIS

the ground is strewn with debris/
the air is thick with hubris (2019) • **@davidbellingham_**

@heyastranaut

 @heyastranaut I find inspiration in literally everything – from contemporary art to new technologies and space missions. Poetry exists all around us, although this depends on one's definition of poetry. My definition is pretty broad, so a poem for me pops up from every corner.

@robertmontgomeryghost

@robertmontgomeryghost Instagram is a very democratic medium, and as an artist, I feel the art system is becoming more democratic because of platforms like Instagram. The art we see is no longer necessarily selected in a top-down way by a small group of curators, and I think that has to be a good thing for the art world.

@depressingfridgepoems

@depressingfridgepoems Literally everything inspires me. Sometimes it'll be a TV show or an article I read, but just as often it's a word or a phrase I come across that triggers something weird in my brain.

What would you wear today
if you knew the world could
not punish you for it?

How much brighter would
this world be if we were
allowed to exist in full.

Today I am dreaming of
pavements filled not with
gold, or pavements that are
empty, rather pavements
full of no one staring -
because we are all too busy
joining in.

@travisalabanza

@travisalabanza I'm inspired by so many things. From pop music videos, to my mother, to love notes, to my loud friends Alok Vaid-Menon and Malik Nashad Sharpe, and fashion and texts.

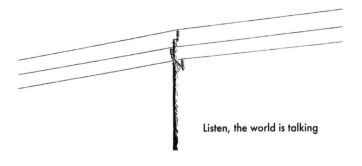

Listen, the world is talking

@textblockcentral

@textblockcentral I often don't have a plan of what I want to make when I create for Instagram – I get a feeling, a call to say something in shapes and colours and words. We turn to poetry when words fail us, and as a poet, I inhabit that wordless void and try to make something out of it.

WHEN THE EARTH BURNED

"Where were you when the earth burned?"
they will ask, and we will explain to them
about Brexit and Trump and Fake News
and billionaires and corporate taxes and big oil
and how it wasn't just the rainforest burning
but Afghanistan and Syria and Yemen
and Kashmir and Sudan were bleeding too
and the ice caps were melting
and the coral reef was dying
and the tigers and leopards
and elephants were going extinct
and *of course,* so many of us were fighting
but the well of truth was poisoned
so strongly and how we did not listen to
the enviornmentalists and scientists on time
because how does one fight monsters
when there are an eternity of them
to fight, we promise, we *promise,* we tried.

"Where were you when the earth burned?"
they will ask, and we will hold our hands out,
take theirs and say, "we too, like you,
were hoping, praying, wishing...
and just trying to survive."

Nikita Gill

When the Earth Burned • **@nikita_gill**

@nikita_gill I'm inspired by reading, walks, the universe, myths and legends, folklore and history. And constant existential crisis.

when you say 'gay'
in place of 'weird'
you forget a child
may be listening

a child who <u>is</u> gay
and afraid to <u>love</u>
because of what
one word means

— sam payne

@bysampayne

@bysampayne I'm incredibly proud to contribute to the poetry community on Instagram, and to offer people like me – LGBTQ+ people, the heartbroken, those that struggle with their mental health – words that make them feel normal and less alone.

IX.

SPIRITUALITY

In an ever-growing digital world, you could argue that we're further from the spiritual than humans have ever been. And yet there remains a persistent exploration among some Instagram poets to represent the intangible, to bring a little divinity to the cacophony of our timelines. Perhaps it makes more sense than we first imagined; that as we worship at the altar of the internet and its holy powers, the metaphysical reaches us in new and different ways. If the imagination really is the 'body of God' as William Blake believed, then perhaps this explains the ethereal presence revealing itself in some of these poems.

[REPETITION]

MY BELIEFS ARE CRUSHED
AMETHYST ROCKS / IN AN
ALTERNATE REALITY/ REPEATING
THINGS WOULD SAVE THEM/
I'D WEAR THE SAME SHIRT
TWICE / I'D SAY FORGIVENESS
IN MY SLEEP / I'D CALL MY
FATHER / HALF OF ME IS A
POET WITH ANAPHORA STUCK IN
MY NAILS / THERE'S VERY LITTLE
CHANCE OF SAVING / EVERYTHING
I LOVE

— NOOR UNNAHAR

@noor_unnahar

@noor_unnahar I think of Instagram as a living journal. When I am not writing and sharing poetry there, it's all about my life as an art student in Karachi. It helps me connect with people on a more human level. My life is out there for them to see, as if a journal is left open.

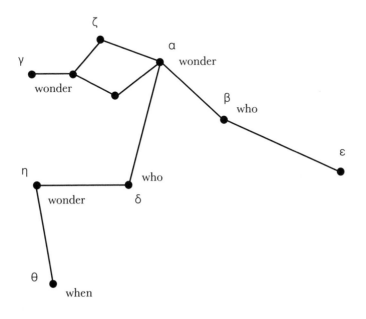

ζ

γ

α wonder

wonder

β who

ε

η

who

wonder δ

θ

when

Station to Station • **@heyastranaut**

@heyastranaut I like to think about social media as a mini universe. An Instagram post, a bit like a star, can travel a long way or can be short-lived, but in the end, it is at the centre of an idiosyncratic system.

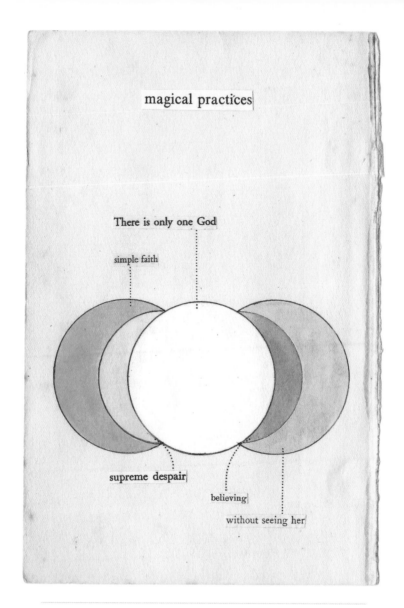

magical practices

There is only one God

simple faith

supreme despair

believing

without seeing her

@diagram_poems

@diagram_poems I'm interested in faith and how we inherit ancient ideas. Through my creative practice I try to deconstruct, critique and rethink the ancient ideas and systems of belief that I was taught to 'take on faith' as I was growing up.

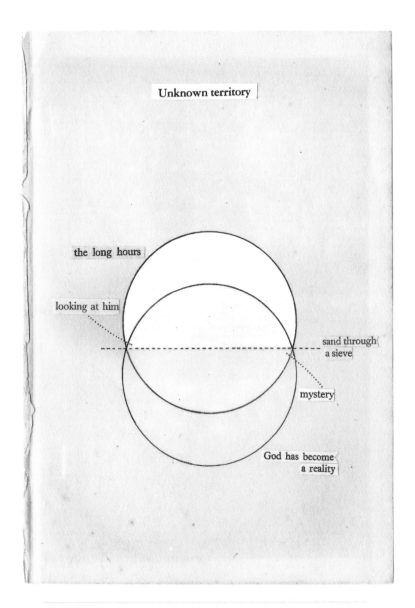

Unknown territory

the long hours

looking at him

sand through
a sieve

mystery

God has become
a reality

@diagram_poems

@diagram_poems I borrow a lot of imagery from Bible stories and theology. I think it is important to look at ideas around faith and religion in the context of everyday life and draw inspiration from events in my life.

hope is a soft kind of prayer, too.

alison malee

@alison.malee

@alison.malee Instagram allows me to play with some of the more visual aspects of my work, such as illustrations, photography etc. It really has challenged me to think outside of words on a page, and pushes me to pour more of myself into my art.

@postpoetical

 @postpoetical I get a lot of inspiration from visual artists and other poets. In fact, you could say that a lot of my work is about inspiration as much as it is about anything else. I like to think of myself as being in conversation with the artists and writers I love, which is probably why I'm so drawn to the collage aspects of Instagram.

@robertmontgomeryghost

@robertmontgomeryghost When I started making my work the internet didn't really exist, at least not in its current accelerated form, and social media certainly didn't exist. Someone told me one day around 2012 that this work had been shared around 10 million times online and I thought that seemed crazy.

@michaelpaulukonis

I imagine there is a
wind, that is blowing
away, but always arriving
at good new birthdays.
Pouring and pouring
transparent stars through
the great surrendering
skies, regressing in
ancient light that
is heavy because it
lugs the dilemma of
ancient light like the
mystery of flowers and
the accidentalness of
ornaments. I watch the
temperature and the low
battery light burn and
wave and go colder in
the thought of emptying
the sink to let life go.
It keeps blowing and
occasionally stopping to
give way to a family or
floating bags of water.
I see a face, it is a face
I love, it pours a kind
of counter-light to the
rest of the strange past
and invisible future. And
it looks like my own
mother carrying anarchic oceans on her back.

Life

@gretabellamacina

@gretabellamacina Nature is liberation, it is home to everyone,
and, like the mind, it continues to develop and renew. When I write
poetry it is usually about the here and the now.

@adrianadrtolivera

@adrianadrtolivera In my childhood, I struggled to express myself in words, so I found images were a way to do that. Even when I create collages that don't contain words, I can see poetry there. In my opinion, images can strike chords in people as much as words can.

X.

WORD PLAY

Just as previous generations of poets have experimented with the written word on the page, Instagram poets have shown flare and rebellion when it comes to creating attention-grabbing works. Letters fall away to reveal a hidden message (or nothing at all), words are hammered across the page, repeated over and over again, or entire words are deliberately forgotten. Despite the square window format of Instagram, these poets are breaking away from the restrictions of the tiles on their profiles, and the results show an affinity with the work of the post-war concrete poetry movement: experimental, highly stylized and most importantly, fun.

A Brok n Po m

Upon b ing awok n
h found his k yboard was brok n.
Th ' ' did not work,
it drov him b rs rk,
h f lt lik a j rk.

So h w nt to s Louis .
Sh was ag r to pl as .
Sh was th b 's kn s.

@brian_bilston

@brian_bilston Instagram helps me to think not just about what to write but also how to present my words. This may be in the form of concrete poetry, or poems in Venn diagrams or Excel spreadsheets – anything that might strengthen the relationship between form and content.

**Poem Interrupted,
written on uncharged iPhone**

Oh dear,
what can the matter be?

My phone
has run out of ba

@brian_bilston

@brian_bilston Lots of things inspire me, most of which could be broadly categorized under the heading 'the absurdity of life'. This would incorporate such varied items as bin collection, bus timetables, office drudgery, and love. But all poetry reflects the time in which it is created, and there may sometimes be a political or social impulse behind my writing.

the solution (2019)   •   **@anatolknotek**

she slides under tubula arches to interrupt the surface of shallow water surrounded by shadows of the future # hypnotising daylight of estuarine habitats convulses into striated articulations

Sea to Spawn • **@heyastranaut**

@heyastranaut Instagram has encouraged me to create new ways of engaging with language due to the abundance of visual-textual material that it offers. I treat my profile as a gallery space – it feels satisfying to be able to curate your own content across one page with its perfectly squared frames.

DOORS DOORS DOORS **CLOSED**
DOORS DOORS DOORS CLOSED
DOORS DOORS DOORS CLOSED
DOORS DOORS DOORS CLOSED
DOORS DOORS DOORS CLOSED
DOORS DOORS DOORS CLOSED
DOORS DOORS DOORS CLOSED
DOORS DOORS DOORS CLOSED
DOORS DOORS DOORS CLOSED
DOORS **KEEP**   DOORS CLOSED
DOORS DOORS DOORS CLOSED
DOORS DOORS DOORS CLOSED
DOORS DOORS **GOING** CLOSED
DOORS DOORS DOORS CLOSED
DOORS DOORS DOORS CLOSED
DOORS DOORS DOORS CLOSED
DOORS DOORS DOORS CLOSED
UNTIL   DOORS DOORS **OPEN**

title: doors

by xie.jin.hao

@xie.jin.hao

@xie.jin.hao I like to share my work as a work in progress so that other people see the flaws in my poems. In return, I hope that encourages people to write poetry. Don't we all need a bit poetry in our lives?

echo echo echo echo echo echo echo echo echo
echo echo echo echo echo echo echo echo echo
echo echo echo echo echo echo echo echo echo
echo echo echo echo echo echo echo echo
echo echo echo echo echo echo echo echo
echo echo echo echo echo echo echo
echo echo echo echo echo echo

@lukebuserart

@lukebuserart I would have to say my biggest inspirations come from experimental and avant-garde music and art.

theTerminal.
in:theMetastasis[coexistencecollides]:
in:theRegister.paradox[theconditioninterfaces]:
to_____Archive_____speechlessness.

theFermentationofAnalog{continuously_
contagious{objectsOfmetaphors};but-do-not-rely-
on-assemblage-to-grow.}

On.loop: 'S[t]aying_alive_requires_aMosaic:
    picnic_blanket;soil;blueprints_for_the_sea:
  picnic_blanket;soil;blueprints_for_the_sea:

@aft3rthought

@aft3rthought Instagram is more accepting towards experimental forms of writing and art that floats between genres; there is less pressure to fit into a category since you are curating your own work. It's a digital exhibition space that allows me to be both a curator and artist.

in my corners

i write

about the things that live
in me

how they play
noughts &

crosses

with dice. with teeth.   i like

the way they sit
on a page. so that i can
touch them

with both hands

@zahrah_s

@zahrah_s Instagram allows me to have fun, to experiment.
Often I build the image, then write in response. It's almost like
painting – or the closest I can get to it as I can't paint or draw.
Using Instagram has made me feel like I can create.

@egysorosok

@egysorosok I love puns. I love to play with words, make a creative joke. Create a picture with few words. My biggest inspiration is this superfast world we are living in, how can I touch someone's soul in that two seconds they spend on my post on Instagram while scrolling down ...

@michaelpaulukonis

 @michaelpaulukonis I wrote an app called 'Polychrome' (it literally means using several colours), which allows me to paint with coloured text. Years ago I wanted to be able to paint with text the way Jackson Pollock dripped and flung his paint – the app allows me to break away from the linear control of the keyboard and escape my own expectations.

Acknowledgements

This book has grown out of the National Poetry Library's Instagram poetry exhibition, which took place from 26 April to 1 July 2018. This was the world's first exhibition of Instagram poetry and included a call-out for people to submit their Instapoems using the National Poetry Library's hashtag #instapoetrylib. The library received over 1,000 submissions and our favourites were chosen for the exhibition, with the top three being invited to perform their work in the library. Some of the poets who were featured in the exhibition are also included in this book.

We would like to thank the National Poetry Library team for their knowledge, enthusiasm and passion for all things poetry. We would also like to thank our colleagues at Southbank Centre, particularly Ted Hodgkinson and Bea Colley in the Literature Team, and the press and marketing departments, who helped to make the exhibition such a success.

Instagram poetry is an ever-evolving genre and you can follow the journey on our Instagram page: @nationalpoetrylibrary and on our website: www.nationalpoetrylibrary.org.uk.

Credits

Pages 13 and 66: © TylerKnott/Tarcher Perigee/Chasersofthelight.com. Pages 14 and 26: Lucy Litman. Pages 15 and 102: Nikita Gill. Pages 16, 39, 60 and 86: Jacqueline Smith. Pages 17, 63, 98 and 112: Robert Montgomery. Pages 18 and 89: Rachel Clift (R. Clift). Pages 20 and 49: poems by Hannah Gordon/illustrations by Michael Cox. Page 24: Maria Mori; original text by Charles Dickens (1859), *A Tale of Two Cities*; photography by Maria Campbell Photography. Pages 25 and 82: Alison A. Malee. Page 27: Ryan Walter Wagner – Vancouver, BC. Page 28: Jon Lupin. Pages 29, 108 and 109: Matthew Kay. Pages 30 and 125: Zahrah Sheikh. Pages 31 and 124: S. Che. Pages 33 and 71: © 2020 Christopher Poindexter. Pages 37 and 72: Ben Maxfield, writer and photographer. Page 41: Kaileigh Pfaff/@kayf.j on instagram, writer and creator of collages. Pages 42, 59, 94 and 120: All works and photos by Anatol Knotek https://www.instagram.com/anatolknotek/. Pages 43 and 64: Pratishtha Khattar. Pages 44 and 91: Zarah M. Burgess. Pages 45, 78, 79 and 100: Travis Alabanza. Pages 48, 118 and 119: © Brian Bilston. Pages 51, 84 and 96: David Bellingham. Pages 52 and 53: Tim Key. Pages 58, 76 and 110: *To Drink Coffee With a Ghost* and *The Mermaid's Voice Returns in This One* © 2019 Amanda Lovelace. Reprinted with Permission of Andrews McMeel Publishing. All rights reserved. Pages 61 and 114: Greta Bellamacina. Page 62: Manuela Beyer-Bunk; poem translated from German to English by Susan Pfenninger; word and sentence generator Jan Bunk. Pages 65 and 88: Marya Layth; 'Static Love' artist Krystina Melville; 'Overgrown' artist Toon Joosen. Pages 67 and 126: Sophie Tari www.egysorosok.com. Pages 70 and 99: Rusty Epstein – artist, author. Page 73: ivy at midnight (Emily Seaton). Page 75: April Hill Writing/Mud Street Publishing. Page 77: Susie LaFond. Pages 85 and 123: Luke Buser. Pages 97, 107 and 121: Astra Papachristodoulou/'No Hope' was showcased at the first Instagram poetry exhibition at the National Poetry Library in June 2018 – I'm grateful to Jessica Atkinson and Chris McCabe for the opportunity to take part in this exciting event. 'Sea to Spawn' was first published in *The Creel* anthology by Guillemot Press, and 'Station to Station' first appeared in the *Europoe* anthology by Kingston University Press. Many thanks to the editors of these publications for their support. Page 103: Sam Payne. Page 106: Noor Unnahar. Pages 113 and 127: © Michael J. Paulukonis. Page 115: Adriana Drt Olívéra.